The Library of
NATIVE AMERICANS

The Pomo
of California

Jack S. Williams

The Rosen Publishing Group's
PowerKids Press™
New York

To Sherman and Essie Adler, who have always had a kind word and interesting questions

Published in 2003 by The Rosen Publishing Group, Inc.
29 East 21st Street, New York, NY 10010

Photo and Illustration Credits: Cover courtesy Beloit College, Logan Museum of Anthropology, Beloit, WI (16516); p. 4 Erica Clendening; p. 7 © Darrell Gulin/CORBIS; pp. 8, 12, 14, 17, 19, 20, 22, 25, 52 courtesy Northwestern University Library; pp. 11, 28 courtesy National Museum of the American Indian, Smithsonian Institution (p. 11, PO3445; p. 28, N31622, photo by Carmelo Guadagno); p. 31 © Christie's Images/CORBIS; pp. 32, 43, 44, 48 © Bettmann/CORBIS; p. 34 © Michael T. Sedam/CORBIS; pp. 37, 38, 47 courtesy Mission San Rafael Arcangel, photos © Cristina Taccone; p. 41 © Dave G. Houser/CORBIS; p. 54 © Robert Holmes/CORBIS.

Book Design: Erica Clendening

Williams, Jack S.
    The Pomo of California / by Jack S. Williams.
        p. cm. — (The library of Native Americans)
    Includes bibliographical references and index.
    Contents: Introducing the Pomo people—Everyday Pomo life—Other features of Pomo life—The Pomo and the newcomers—The twentieth century—The Pomo today.
        ISBN 0-8239-6436-1
        1. Pomo Indians—Juvenile literature. [1. Pomo Indians. 2. Indians of North America—California.] I. Title. II. Series.
    E99.P65 W55 2002   2002-006615
    979.4'0049757—dc21

Manufactured in the United States of America

There are a variety of terminologies that have been employed when writing about Native Americans. There are sometimes differences between the original language used by a Native American group for certain names or vocabulary and the anglicized or modernized versions of such names or terms. Although this book contains terms that we feel will be most recognizable to our readership, there may also exist synonymous or native words that are preferred by certain speakers.

Contents

The Pomo and Their Neighbors

Athapaskan

Pacific
Ocean

Yuki

Wintun

Pomo

Patwin

Area of Detail

Nevada

California

Wappo

Coast
Miwok

San Francisco

One

Introducing the Pomo People

The gray fog of early morning covers the coastal mountains and hills of Northern California with a great blanket of silence. Giant redwood trees reach into the sky like a thousand cathedrals. To the east of the coastal mountains are valleys, lakes, and hills covered by grasslands and oak forests. This beautiful land is the home of the Pomo. They are a Native American nation with many faces. During their long history, the Pomo have included warriors, hunters, fishermen, craftspeople, and traders. The story of their triumph is filled with courage and determination.

The Pomos' ancient lands include parts of modern Mendocino, Sonoma, and Lake Counties. Although many of the native people lived at sea level, they routinely passed through the highest peaks, which reached more than 6,560 feet (2 km). The climate of the coastal area was wet and cold. Although snow was relatively rare, rainstorms were common. Between 40 to 50 inches (100 to 127 cm) of rain fell each year. Even when it was not raining, a cold fog often settled on the land. The Pomo who lived in the valleys to the east of the coastal peaks faced fewer challenges. The summers there are comparatively hot and the winters relatively mild and dry.

This map shows the homeland of the Pomo, in present-day California.

The earliest known writings to mention the Pomo appeared about 1851, when Colonel Redick McKee referred to the people living on the Russian River as Pomos. Many people think that the word was a native term for a particular village. It means "at red earth hole."

The early Pomo divided themselves into seven smaller nations. Most modern scholars label these nations the Northern Pomo, Northeastern Pomo, Eastern Pomo, Southeastern Pomo, Central Pomo, Southern Pomo, and Southeastern Pomo. Each of these people had their own language, customs, and traditions. Because their languages had many similar features, scholars have grouped all of them together as Pomo. Prior to contact with outsiders, the seven groups did not describe themselves as a single nation. However, since 1851, most of them call themselves Pomo.

No one knows when the first member of this group appeared. Most researchers agree that between 40,000 and 13,000 years ago, people from Asia came to North America across a frozen land bridge that stretched from Alaska to Siberia. During the thousands of years that followed, these first immigrants to the Americas slowly moved south.

Around 8,000 years ago, some of the nations had moved into the coastal areas of present-day California. The region that lay to the north of Bodgea Bay was filled with towering mountains, redwood forests, swift streams, and thundering rivers. Over time, the ancestors of the Pomo learned how to use the natural resources that they found. They gradually developed their own types of tools, customs, languages, and beliefs.

Estimates by modern scholars suggest that in 1800 there were probably more than 8,000 Pomo. Since that time, Native Americans faced many challenges to their existence and way of life. Invasions of their land by Russia were followed by those from Spain, Mexico, and finally the United States. As more and more newcomers came, the Pomo, along with other Native Americans, were killed or pushed aside. By 1900, the Pomo had lost control of nearly all of their lands. Throughout their many conflicts with the newcomers, these Native Americans tried to resist invasion. Today, the Pomo are still fighting for their fair treatment and civil rights.

The redwood forests were an important resource for the Pomo.

7

Two

Everyday Pomo Life

When Europeans reached the Pomo lands, they discovered a people who were experts at using the many natural resources that surrounded them. They were skilled woodsmen, fishermen, and craftspeople. The Pomo had unique styles of houses, tools, and artwork.

Living with Nature

The Pomo relied on the natural world for everything that they ate, wore, and used as tools. The land was rich in edible plants, including acorns, buckeyes, and many nutritious berries, roots, nuts, and seeds. The men were expert hunters. They brought home many large animals, such as elks, sea lions, and bears, as well as smaller creatures, such as rabbits and even insects. The ocean, lakes, rivers, and streams provided many other foods. The Pomo enjoyed dining on large amounts of salmon. They ate many other kinds of fish, shellfish, and even sea plants, such as kelp.

All kinds of plants and animals were also used to make tools and crafts. The Pomo depended on many kinds of stones and minerals for their survival. Salt was collected from the shoreline and from natural deposits in the interior. Rocks of various kinds were

In this 1924 photo by Edward S. Curtis, a Pomo man gazes over the shores of Clear Lake.

fashioned into tools and beads. Hematite, a red mineral, was used as paint. The Pomos' weapons included bows, slings, clubs, and spears. A *bola* is a weapon that the Pomo made by tying stones to both ends of a long piece of leather. *Bolas* were thrown into the air to kill birds, such as geese. The natives also used nets, brush fences, and even special basket traps to catch game.

The Pomos' ideas about nature were very different from the beliefs held by most early Europeans. For example, many natives taught their children that it was very important that people limit how much food they took from the earth. Pomo traditions required them to respect the value of other forms of life and even of the land itself.

Despite their noble ideas and teachings, the Pomo still suffered many problems and hardships. It was not always easy to live by hunting and gathering. There were disastrous fires, storms, diseases, droughts, and other catastrophes. Some Pomo were greedy or jealous of their neighbors. They fought wars against each other, and other Native Americans, over the control of resources, such as land. While the early Pomo often enjoyed a peaceful existence in a world of plenty, they also faced conflict and turmoil.

Clothing and Body Decoration

Despite the challenging weather conditions found in the Pomo's territory, the men and small children often wore little or no clothing. Many males wore short skirts, or breechcloths. A breechcloth is made from a single piece of cloth or hide that was passed between the legs and tied to a belt at both ends. Pomo women always wore a skirt that covered the area from their waist to their ankles.

This photo from the early twentieth century depicts a Pomo man in traditional ceremonial clothing.

They also wore short capes that completely covered their upper bodies. Some of the Pomo wore reed shoes, leggings, hairnets, and sweatbands.

When the weather was cold, some women wore two skirts, and most people wrapped themselves in blankets. When it rained, everyone pro-

tected themselves with capes made from skins, shredded reeds, or tree bark. Other kinds of clothing were worn on special occasions. When the men hunted deer, they often wore elaborate masks and skins that made them look like animals. During ceremonies, some men wore feather robes and sashes, or belts, as well as elaborate headdresses made from feathers, plants, fur, and jewelry. Some rituals called for people to wear body paint.

This 1924 photo depicts a Pomo woman preparing food outside of her home, a summer camp at Lake Pomo.

Most Pomo liked to wear jewelry. Some of their favorite items were shell or stone beads, which were frequently woven into belts, neckbands and wristbands, and earrings made from wood and bone. Shell pendants and feather ornaments were also popular. The jewelry that a person owned often reflected his or her wealth and importance within a village community. The more beads and related items that a person had, the richer and more important he or she was.

After 1800, the Pomo adopted many items of European-style clothing. Glass beads and various kinds of metal ornaments were popular. The Pomo often combined the new materials with the old ones in creative ways.

Villages

There were many villages contained within each of the seven Pomo regions. These communities ranged in size from as few as a dozen houses to more than 100. The populations of the larger settlements sometimes included more than 1,000 people. The village structures were usually spread out over a large area along the sides of a creek or river, with as much as 300 feet (90 m) separating houses. The larger communities often covered more than two miles (3 km).

Each village was made up of many homes. The Pomo created their homes in different styles, depending where they lived. In many coastal areas, homes were built using heavy logs and slabs of redwood bark. The Pomo who lived to the east of the redwood forests built their houses out of willow poles, brush, grass, and reeds.

The redwood houses had round floor plans and pointed roofs that looked like short cones. Most of these homes measured 8 to 15 feet (2.5 to 4.5 m) across, and 6 to 8 feet (2 to 2.5 m) high. These structures provided protection for a family, which usually included a mother, a father, children, grandparents, and at least a few aunts and uncles. Some structures may have housed as many as twelve people. People could enter the houses through a low doorway.

The Pomo made canoes out of reeds to navigate rivers and streams.

The Pomo who lived to the east of the redwood forests built a style of home that could shelter several related families. More than thirty people could live under one roof. The homes were circular, oval, rectangular, and L-shaped. The larger houses could measure over 40 feet (12 m) across and about 12 feet (3.5 m) tall. To build these structures, a series of thin willow poles were tied together to create a frame. The frame was usually covered by bundles of reeds or grass. Many of the large homes had several doors. Most of these houses looked like an upside-down bowl.

Inside the Pomos' homes, there was a hearth, or fire pit, that was usually created near the center of the room. In some of the larger homes, there were several hearths. The flames warmed the people when it was cold and allowed them to cook food indoors during bad weather. A hole in the center of the roof allowed light to enter and smoke to escape into the sky. Most Pomo preferred to prepare their meals out of doors. Some big homes had room for women to grind acorns into flour. The families' property, which included things such as baskets, was stored inside their homes.

Every Pomo village had a sweathouse, where men would take sweat baths. Sweathouses were round structures built inside a pit. A layer of earth was often thrown on the roofs to make them more air-tight. The Pomo lit a fire inside, filling the space with smoke and heat. Men took daily sweat baths for cleansing, healing, and enjoyment. In some communities, the males slept and spent most of their free time in the sweathouse.

Every village had at least one assembly house. These structures were also built inside a large pit. Assembly houses were used for many different kinds of ceremonies and meetings. Most of them were round, and some measured more than 70 feet (21 m) in diameter. The heavy roofs were held up by an elaborate system of painted wooden columns. Some assembly houses were also covered by earth. Many had a long entrance tunnel at their south end. Light flooded into the rooms through a central opening in the roof. At the north end of the assembly house, a section of the wall was designed to be pushed away to allow for a quick escape in case of an emergency, such as a fire.

Most of the Pomo spent at least part of the year in campsites located away from their main village. They set up temporary settlements in places where food became available. Most of the shelters at the campsites were made of poles and thatch.

Cooking

The women used a variety of methods to prepare food. Some foods, such as acorns and buckeyes, had to be ground into flour and soaked for many hours in fresh water to remove poisonous substances. Many kinds of dried fish and shellfish also had to be hammered into powder before they were ready to be cooked. There were many plants and seeds that could be eaten without any preparation.

Most dishes were cooked over an open flame. Some foods were grilled, smoked, or steamed. The early Pomo were experts at cooking stews inside tightly woven baskets using hot rocks. The Pomo prepared many meals in simple ovens that they built in the ground. To make an oven, they dug a hole in the ground and built a fire inside. After a while, the fuel was removed to put out the fire, leaving the rocks and soil hot enough to cook the food. The food, which was usually wrapped in leaves, was put inside the pit. The hole was then filled with hot rocks. After a few hours, the dish was ready to be eaten.

Pictured here are Pomo baskets used to gather and sift seeds and nuts.

Pomo preserved all of their leftover food for later use or trade. For example, they salted or smoked almost every kind of fish and meat to prevent it from spoiling. Acorns and dried plant foods were stored in baskets or similar containers.

Other Arts and Crafts

Every Pomo village had people who were experts at making beautiful crafts and useful tools. Obsidian, a volcanic glasslike rock, was skillfully chipped into arrowheads, drills, knives, and various other cutting tools. The surfaces of red magnesite rocks were smoothed to make magnificent beads. The Pomo, like most Native Americans, relied on stone as one of their most important resources. Pomo craftspeople shaped stones into useful tools, such as pestles and mortars. The pestles were long stone cylinders, and the mortars were rocks with large, round holes. The women used mortars and pestles to grind acorns and seeds into flour. Sometimes dozens of holes were made in a rocky outcropping. The outcroppings were called bedrock mortars.

The Pomo made many useful things from the animals that they hunted. Skins were transformed into clothing and blankets. Bones were crafted into awls, jewelry, and fishhooks. Dozens of different things were made from seashells and bird feathers.

The plant kingdom provided craftspeople with other raw materials. The women collected many different kinds of grass, rushes, and shoots to weave into baskets. The baskets were decorated with intricate geometric patterns. Beads and feathers were sometimes added to their compositions for additional decoration. Many different types and sizes of baskets were produced, including hoppers, plates, bowls, jars, and miniatures. Many experts believe that the Pomo created, and continue to make, the finest baskets on Earth.

Wood, bark, and reeds were also used to make hundreds of different kinds of useful things, such as bows, cloth, and smoking pipes. In order to reach nearby coastal islands, Pomo men tied driftwood logs together to create simple rafts. The people who lived to the east of the redwoods tied bundles of reeds together to make swift boats. Many Pomo vessels measured more than 13 feet (4 m) in length.

Pictured here are Pomo baskets, a mortar, and a pestle. These utensils were important items used by the Pomo for food preparation and storage.

Three

Other Features of Pomo Life

The early Pomo were different from Europeans and other Native Americans in several other important ways. They had their own languages, social structure, systems of government, warfare, trade, and religious beliefs.

Language

Each of the seven Pomo nations had their own language. Because they shared certain words and other features, scholars believe that all seven languages were a part of the same family. Within each of the Pomo languages, a number of different versions of the languages, called dialects, were also spoken.

Social Structure

Every community has some form of social structure. A social structure provides a way of dividing up people into groups and assigning them special jobs. Among the Pomo, people were assigned to groups based on whether they were men or women, who their parents were, their age, their wealth, and what they had accomplished.

In this photo, a Pomo woman is wearing a large burden basket, suspended from her forehead by a cord called a trump line. The photograph was taken by Edward S. Curtis around 1924.

The smallest Pomo social groups were extended families. Newly married couples could move near either the wife or husband's family. Some men had more than one wife. It was relatively easy for a married couple to get divorced. The average family had about fourteen people. The jobs around the house were

22   In this photo, a Pomo woman is gathering reeds. These items were especially important to groups that lived along the shorelines of lakes.

usually assigned according to a person's age and gender. Several extended families were usually united into a single larger group that was headed by the oldest family members. Most villages included several larger family units.

Most of the Pomo men, and many women, worked at a single full-time job. Besides leaders and doctors, there were bead makers, hunters, basket makers, bow and arrow makers, and many other specialists. Each group formed its own trade organization. Scholars have sometimes called these groups secret societies. A person had to study many years before he or she was allowed to join or to practice without supervision. The wealthiest and most powerful men were the political leaders, often called chiefs. A second important group included the religious and medical leaders. Among these people, the bear doctors, who could be either men or women, were the most powerful.

Government

The basic unit of government of the Pomo was the village community. Some scholars have called these groups tribelets. Each of the seven original nations had their own lands and a central settlement. The largest nation may have included as many as 2,000 members, and may have contained a number of smaller, independent villages.

The system of government of each of the seven early Pomo nations was not the same. In some communities there was a single major leader, or chief. In other Pomo villages, the chiefs had several aides.

The Pomo of California

The leaders sometimes inherited their positions, while others were elected by the nation's adults. In some communities, the oldest people from each extended family came together with others to form a village council, or assembly. The Central Pomo had the most complicated system of government, with two main chiefs, a war captain, seven men who spoke on behalf of the assembly houses, and a number of assistant leaders.

The village officials served as the Pomo's judges and police. They also organized the religious ceremonies and led the people during times of crisis. The position of chief, or other kinds of leader, was usually inherited. Most chiefs were men, although some women who were chief's daughters or sisters, also held important positions. Most of the time, the leaders did not try to tell their followers what to do. Both men and women enjoyed a great deal of freedom. If someone objected to their chief's behavior, they often moved into another community.

The different Pomo villages sometimes formed temporary alliances. A few of the leaders had control of several villages for short periods of time. However, these alliances most often quickly broke down.

Every Pomo community had its own territory for hunting and gathering. Anyone who entered these areas without permission could be attacked. The resources that were contained within some of the Pomos' lands were divided between those shared by the group as a whole and those owned by individuals. Among other groups, no individual owned land. It was all shared by the community.

This photograph of a Pomo elder was taken in 1924.

25

Warfare

Warfare was important to the early Pomo. The men of each village served as warriors who protected their community's property and rights. Conflicts were caused by many different problems. Villagers often fought over the control of natural resources, such as fishing areas. Other wars took place when the religious leaders of one community performed rituals designed to hurt another. Once one side had been defeated or hurt, the other side often sought revenge.

When it was clear that a war was coming, the men would begin to prepare for battle. The warriors held religious ceremonies in which they prayed and worshiped with special dances and songs. The religious leaders tried to use supernatural powers to predict what would happen during the fighting. Some men believed that they could also predict what would happen through their dreams.

Sometimes a war was settled by a ritual battle in which two armies came together at a designated place to trade insults and arrows. As soon as someone was killed, the war ended. The losers had to give up something in exchange for peace. A victorious group of warriors sometimes celebrated their success with special ceremonies.

The Pomo also fought more violent forms of war. Both sides would use ambushes, or secret attacks. Women and children, who were peacefully collecting food, were often captured or killed. Sometimes the winners would destroy the opponents' entire village.

More often than not, the victors peacefully met with their enemy after the war to make an agreement. Usually the losers had to pay the winners for ending the conflict.

Trade

Most of the items that the Pomo required could be found near their villages and campsites. They obtained other raw materials by trading with their neighbors or more distant Native American nations. Trade helped the Pomo to develop friendly relations and encouraged peace among the Native Americans who lived throughout Northern California.

Sometimes the people of one village would invite the entire population of another settlement to come for a trade visit. When the visitors arrived to exchange or sell things, the hosts would hold a big party that could go on for several days. When they were not eating, the visitors and hosts often gambled or took sweat baths together. Many people would give their friends gifts. Sometimes, individuals from different groups would decide to get married. The family ties between nations helped to create and strengthen connections between different villages. When one area had a food shortage, their trading partners often invited them for a visit to give them food.

The Pomo exchanged many things, including salt, meat, fish, acorns, hides, arrow tips, bows, basketry materials, and magnesite.

The Pomo of California

The black glass called obsidian, which was found near volcanoes, was particularly valuable. The owners of different resources sometimes rented the use of their lands to outsiders in exchange for trade goods.

The Pomo often used beads made from clamshells and magnesite as a kind of money. Later, European goods such as glass beads and metal tools were also used in native trade and payments. By counting bead money, the Pomo developed amazing mathematical skills.

These photos show a circular, feathered gift basket.

Religion

Religion was an important part of most Pomos' lives. It helped them to make sense of the world and learn what they should do to be good people. Some of the elders spoke of the wise God, Madunda, who lived in the sky. His younger brother, who figured in many religious stories, was a playful coyote, known simply as Coyote. Coyote did many things, including creating the first people. One story began when he learned that some people had mistreated his sons. As a result, he decided to set a fire that would burn up the whole world. A spider came out of the skies and rescued Coyote and his family. Later, Coyote returned to the earth. Coyote became thirsty and drank water until his belly was completely filled. A Pomo holy man suddenly appeared and jumped on the animal's stomach. This caused the water to pour out, covering everything and putting out the fire.

Most Pomo holidays and rituals were connected to their faith. From the time that they were born, young people were taught songs, dances, and religious stories. There were many ceremonies for boys and girls that marked special occasions as they grew up. There were also many beautiful services that marked the passing of the seasons. Special ceremonies were held to bring the Pomo power, health, and good fortune. There were many different religious groups within the community who performed their own rituals, such as the healing ceremonies of the bear doctors. The early Pomo believed that certain places were especially important to their religion. Today, these locations are known as prayer rocks. Unlike other Native Americans, the Pomo did not mark the rocks with any special symbols.

Pomo religious leaders spent much of their time working as doctors. Their treatments often combined giving sick people herbs and performing rituals, special songs, and dances. People paid the doctors in goods or bead money. Religious leaders inherited their positions from their parents, or they had a special dream that told them to become leaders. Some doctors were feared because they were said to be able to hurt people with poisons. The Pomos continue to practice their religion to this day.

This photo is of a Pomo gift basket.

Four

The Pomo and the Newcomers (1542–1900)

Between 1542 and 1812, the ships of many different European countries sailed by the Pomo lands. These expeditions included those of Juan Rodriguez Cabrillo, in 1542, and Francis Drake, in 1579. Many of the early ships were Spanish merchant vessels traveling from the Philippines to Mexico. After 1790, there were also voyagers from Portugal, France, and Great Britain. When they wrote about their voyages, these sailors did not mention most of the California Native Americans, including the Pomo. Throughout the Americas, contact with Europeans introduced horrible diseases that may have killed as many as 95 percent of Native Americans. It is likely that the Pomo suffered many deaths when European-introduced illnesses spread from Native American groups to the south and east. By the time that the Europeans came to stay in the Pomo territory in 1812, the size of the population had probably gone down, and then increased, as it had in much of North America.

The Pomo and the Russians

After 1750, things began to change dramatically for all the California Native Americans. Spain and Russia began to put into effect their plans for expansion into North America, which they considered to be

Sir Francis Drake, pictured here, was an English explorer. He was one of the first Europeans to visit the area of the Pomo.

an "empty" region. When Spanish settlers invaded California in 1769, the northernmost center of their colonizing efforts was San Francisco, which was far to the south of the Pomo homeland. The Russians were the first to come into contact with the Pomo. They established a fort called Fort Ross on the California coast in 1812, at the place the Native Americans called Mad-Shiu-Miu.

The Russians built Fort Ross for a number of reasons. They wanted to collect as many sea otter and seal skins as they could from the California coast. The Russians also wanted to create farms and ranches.

Fort Ross became an important post of the Russian American Fur Company. This was one of the first places where the Pomo got to know people from Europe.

They needed food for their outposts in Alaska and the Far East. Although they came in the name of the Russian Empire, the people who established Fort Ross were not interested in controlling California the way that the Spanish were. More than anything else, they wanted to make money. When they arrived, they were happy to pay rent to the local Pomo people in exchange for the use of about 2 square miles (5 square km) of their territory.

At first the Russians and the Pomo got along well. A small group of natives learned Russian. A few became Orthodox Christians. A small number of Pomo women even married the newcomers. The Pomo found the Russians to be good trading partners and military allies. The presence of the Russians helped to keep the Spaniards and other enemy Native Americans far away.

Relations between the Pomo and the Russians were poisoned after 1830, when Fort Ross's troops forced Native Americans to work for them without pay. In 1834, a Russian officer described how his men would capture Pomo and tie their hands behind their backs, then force them to work in the fields.

In 1841, the company that owned Fort Ross, the Russian American Fur Company, decided that the cost of keeping the colony was greater than the profits it was making. The Russians decided to abandon the outpost and sold the buildings to Mexican government officials. Throughout their stay, the Russians had not influenced, or even visited, the vast majority of the Pomos. The Pomos, who had once seen the Russians as allies and partners, were without a doubt glad to see them depart.

The Pomo and the Missions

In 1769, King Carlos III of Spain sent an army to take control of California. Before 1817, the Spanish colonists had focused their efforts on the coastline from San Diego to San Francisco. After the creation of Mission San Rafael among the Miwok Native Americans living on the coast, things began to change. The southern Pomo groups found themselves confronted by Spaniards for the first time.

The Spanish government wanted to block the Russians and expand their control of California. However, they did not have the soldiers, money, or colonists that would have made it possible for them to simply conquer and occupy the region. The officials knew that they would have to form a friendship with at least some of the Native Americans. The California missions were built as communities where Spain's Native American allies would gradually adopt the Christian religion and European way of life. Franciscan priests were placed in charge of the missions.

By the time that Mission San Rafael was created in 1817, the Spanish government had already begun to get rid of the other Franciscan settlements. The people who ran the government had decided that the mission system did not work well, and that it was not right that church officials should be in the position of running the Indian settlements. The mission program in Mexico, which California was a part of, came to an end when the country became independent in 1821. Shortly afterward, Mexican officials put a stop to the missions because they were opposed to the part that the Franciscans had played in Spanish colonization. Nevertheless, Spain granted resources to create Mission San Francisco Solano de Sonoma in 1823. The government approved both San Rafael and Sonoma as a direct result of their lack of other resources to colonize California, and their fear of the Russians.

As early as 1817, some Southern Pomo had decided to move to Mission San Rafael. Over the next eighteen years, at least 600 members of the northern nation moved to missions. However, they

Mission San Rafael brought some Pomo people into the Spanish mission system.

represented only a small part of the population of San Rafael and Sonoma, which was made up mostly of other Native American peoples, particularly the Miwok. The vast majority of the Pomo did not know the missionaries or other colonists.

We do not know what life was like for the Pomo who lived at the missions. Some scholars suggest that they were treated well,

Dozens of books were used to instruct the Pomo, and also to record important facts about them. These book pages can be found at Mission San Rafael Arcangel.

and others have stated that their lives were very difficult. We also do not know how Pomos of that time viewed the struggles between the Russians and the Spaniards.

The Pomo as a whole could not have ignored the changes that were taking place throughout their homeland. By 1823, Europeans and natives from other far away parts of North America frequently passed through Pomo lands, bringing new ideas, trade goods, and diseases. The visitors' horses, cattle, sheep, and goats often escaped and moved into the natives' valleys. Although the new animals provided food, they ate many of the plants that the Pomos gathered for food and drove away animals that they hunted. Some of the new beasts ate every last blade of grass from the hills. Soon, the bare ground began to wash away, flooding streams with mud and creating landslides. Everywhere, the natural balances of humans, plants, and animals that existed for hundreds of years began to collapse. The land itself seemed to be poisoned by the newcomers. Nothing as terrible as this had ever happened before. No one knew exactly what to do to make things better.

We will never know how far the missions might have gone in changing the Pomo way of life. The weak government support for the Franciscans came to an end in 1835. In 1822, the Mexican government began to grant a number of private ranches to retired soldiers. In place of the missions, the new ranches would give Mexico its hold on California. Mission San Rafael and Mission San Francisco Solano de Sonoma were quickly transformed into new kinds of frontier outposts.

Conflict with Mexican Ranchers

The period after 1835 saw many changes in California. The system of government broke down, and wealthy landowners fought with each other over who would rule. Native Americans who lived at the missions became foreigners in the lands of their birth. The ranchers treated the Native Americans much worse than they were treated at the missions. The ranchers saw no future for the Native Americans except as slaves. This tragic belief came from a combination of their desire to steal the natives' lands, and their fear that the Native Americans would somehow rise up and take revenge. Christian Native Americans were once protected by the mission, but soon, many Mexican ranchers captured both Christian and non-Christian Native Americans to use as unpaid workers on their property.

South of San Francisco, many of the Native Americans from the missions escaped to the east, where they joined with other Native Americans and organized their own raiding parties. Between 1835 and 1847, they stole thousands of horses and cattle from the Mexican towns and ranches. Many of the settlements had to be abandoned, and it looked as if the natives might win the struggle.

Native Americans on the northern frontier did not experience the same success as those in the south. Changes in government policies saw the transformation of Sonoma into a military outpost ruled by the brilliant commander Mariano Guadalupe Vallejo.

As commander general of the northern frontier, he wanted to block the Russians and conquer the Pomo. In order to expand Mexican control, he granted ranch after ranch to his followers and family members. In the summer of 1837, Salvador Vallejo led the first major campaign aimed at conquering Pomo territory. By the end of the next year, the newcomers had occupied all of the southern and central Pomo regions. After the abandonment of Fort Ross in 1841, Vallejo and his men continued to organize raids deep into the surrounding

Native American territory. The captives that they brought back were often sold to other ranchers.

The Pomo soon encountered other invaders. Native Americans from as far away as Oregon were attacking people throughout Northern California. Striking without warning, they carried away anyone that they could capture to be sold as slaves to other Native Americans living on the Columbia River. Because they did not keep

This mansion in Sonoma, California was built by Mariano Vallejo. Vallejo was an important figure in Pomo/Mexican race relations during the later part of the nineteenth century.

records, no one knows how many Pomo disappeared during this period as a result of these attacks.

The presence of so many newcomers also helped to spread European diseases. In 1837, a smallpox epidemic broke out and killed many of the Pomo who had managed to escape capture by the Mexicans, the Russians, and other Native Americans.

Between 1835 and 1847, many Pomo died while fighting, or a result of harsh treatment or diseases. Thousands of others became slaves. Many of the Pomo communities somehow managed to hang on. However, the hard times had just begun.

The Pomo and the United States, 1848–1900

The Mexican-American War of 1846–1848 concluded with a treaty that forced Mexico to transfer control of California to the United States. Things did not improve for the Native Americans under the new government. Most American officials believed that all the Native Americans should be eliminated.

The California Gold Rush of 1849 brought tens of thousands of fortune seekers to the region. Although there was no gold to be found in the Pomo area, the settlers soon found other resources that they wanted. Many of the leaders of their government told them that they had a right to take whatever they wanted from the Pomo, whom they called "savages."

During the period from 1850 through 1900, nearly all the Pomo lands were stolen. The Native Americans were never able to organize a common defense to stop the settlers. When individual Pomo villages defended themselves against the outsiders, those who resisted were often hunted down and executed by the U.S. Army or the police.

In 1850, Governor Peter Burnett argued that all remaining Native Americans in California should be exterminated. That same

In this photo, a prospector pans for gold in northern California.

year, a group of United States Cavalry arrived at Clear Lake to investigate the deaths of two ranchers. Charles Stone and Andrew Kelsey had captured many Pomo and forced them to work as slaves on their ranch. After more than a dozen Native Americans died, some of the Pomo killed the two men and fled into the mountains.

Captain Nathaniel Lyon led his horsemen deep into Pomo territory. At a place called Badonnapoti, he found a group of 200 to 300 natives who were peacefully fishing. When their leader, Ge-Wil-Lih, attempted to approach the Americans in friendship he was shot down. Gunfire, sabers, and bayonets were used on the unarmed men, women, and children. Surviving Pomo stated that a few

Peter Burnett, governor of California, had few good things to say about the California Native Americans.

of the captured natives were burned alive. Today, the place is known as Bloody Island.

After the events at Clear Lake, Lyon's men moved to the west toward Ukiah, attacking and killing other Native Americans. Over 150 Pomo men, women, and children were killed. The next year, Colonel Redick McKee signed a peace treaty with some of the Pomo. However, the government backed out of the agreement. It promised to build a reservation to protect the Native Americans, but the reservation was never established.

Eventually, many of the defeated Pomo were forced to live at the bleak Mendocino Indian Reserve near Fort Bragg, and the equally unpleasant place known as the Round Valley Reserve. Many moved to these places because they had nowhere else to go. Meanwhile, the government gave the Pomos' property to the invaders.

In desperation, some of the Native Americans begged the new owners to let them live on their old lands. In exchange for working for almost no wages, some of the Pomo were allowed to live outside of the government reserves. The new communities were called *rancherías*, a Spanish term that had been used for similar native villages throughout California.

Life for all of California's Native Americans remained difficult. The government denied nearly all Native American people, including the Pomo, their basic human rights. A series of harsh laws were passed that allowed local officials to imprison Native

Americans and then to make them work for free. Sometimes wealthy landowners rented the workers from the police.

Despite these horrible things, many of the Pomo preserved their ancient ways. When they were not working on the farms and ranches, they could still be seen hunting, trapping, and fishing. The ancient faith of the Native Americans continued to be practiced, despite the growing numbers of Christian missionaries who attempted to get them to adopt their religion. Many of the Pomo who joined churches also preserved all or part of their older beliefs.

After 1870, many Pomo became involved with the Ghost Dance religion. This faith taught that by following certain rituals, all the newcomers in North America would leave, and the old world would be restored. Unfortunately for the Pomo, the people who had taken their lands did not leave. Despite the failure of the new religion, Pomo parents still taught their children to be faithful to their ancient ways. Pomo beliefs were even combined with some of the new ideas in a creative way to form the Bole Maru religion that still exists. In part, the religion emphasized the ability of people to renew themselves and the land through proper actions and worship.

As the nineteenth century came to an end, many Pomo saved enough money to purchase land, and recreate parts of their old communities, including Coyote Valley, Pinoleville, Yokaya, Potter Valley, Sherwood, and Yorkville. Although legal complications soon threatened most of these new settlements, it was clear that the Pomo were ready to face a new stage in their fight for survival.

These ceramics date from the pre-1835 period. The blue and white pieces are tin-glazed earthenware (*maiolica*) from Puebla (Mexico). The orange pieces are from lead-glazed cooking wares, probably from western Mexico.

Five

The Twentieth Century

By the beginning of the twentieth century, some things had begun to improve for the Pomo. The outsiders' hatred toward them had begun to decline. Some of the Christian missionaries began to join the Pomo's struggle for civil rights. The Native Americans were now using the courts to fight injustice. The Pomo had never given up their pride, and they began to work harder than ever for their rights.

In 1907, a Pomo man, Ethan Anderson, walked into the office of the Lake County Clerk to register to vote. He was refused because he was a Native American. Anderson sued the county, and eventually the Supreme Court of California agreed with him. After this case, all the male Native Americans in California who did not live on reservations were given the right to vote.

After 1910, United States government officials began a new policy of working to create reservations for the homeless Native Americans of California. Fifty-two tiny new communities would be created during the next ten years, including a number of Pomo *rancherías*.

Throughout the period between 1865 and 1950, the Pomos often found it necessary to fight for their right to an education. Young Native Americans were taken from their homes by government

Eleven-year-old Ricky Parrish gazes at Senator Robert F. Kennedy's autograph, which the senator wrote for him during his tour of a Pomo Indian village in January 1967.

officials, sometimes by force, and sent to live at certain schools only for Native Americans. There, they were not allowed to speak native languages or observe traditional customs. They were taught that they had to be like European Americans and disregard their own traditions. After 1900, some Pomo began to fight back. By 1911, the Northern California Indian Association had begun to work to provide better education for the natives. In 1923, the members of the California Indian Brotherhood successfully sued the local Ukiah schools that would not admit Native American pupils. Eventually, things changed and the Native Americans were allowed to go to school with everybody else.

After World War I ended in 1918, Pomo continued their protests over how they, and other Native Americans, were being treated. They demanded that everyone be given the same rights. Pomo voices were heard in the Society of Northern California Indians and the Indian Board of Cooperation. These groups fought for Native Americans' rights. People began to recognize Pomo political leaders, such as Steve Parrish, William Benson, and Stephen Knight. They showed that Native Americans could rise up and take control over their lives, and make the government change the way it treated the Pomo people. Finally, in 1924, the Pomo, along with other Native Americans, were granted the full benefits of United States citizenship, including the right to vote.

Between 1930 and 1941, the Pomo communities, like those of other Americans, suffered through the Great Depression. Everywhere in the United States there was a shortage of jobs and money. Native leaders worked together with government officials to improve the lives of the Pomo. Despite discrimination, more and more Native Americans joined with the larger community of Americans, taking on new jobs and finding friends who faced similar challenges. Many Pomo married people of European, Latin American, and Asian heritages.

The war years of 1941 to 1945 saw many Pomo joining the United States armed forces. After World War II ended, the Native Americans faced a series of new challenges. Some government officials wanted to eliminate the reservation system. The lack of government support threatened to make it more difficult for many Pomo to preserve their culture. In 1966, the government eliminated a number of reservations and divided the lands among their residents. Once again, the Pomo organized themselves to preserve and protect their rights. They joined organizations such as the American Indian Movement that fought unfair conditions and treatment. Tilly Hardwicke, a member of the Pinoleville Pomo, sued the government over its dishonest attempt to eliminate her community as a reservation. In 1983, the courts ruled in favor of Hardwicke, and a total of seventeen reservations were restored.

Six

The Pomo Today

Today, the Pomo see a brighter future. In 1990, 4,900 people identified themselves as members of this proud nation. Pomo live on small reservations at Cloverdale, Dry Creek, Stewarts Point, Lytton, Robinson, Upper Lake, Big Lake, Hoplands, Guidville, Sherwood Valley, Manchester-Point Arena, Round Valley, Pinoleville, Scotts Valley, Potter Valley, Middletown, Grindstone, and Elem-Sulphur Bank. The Coyote Valley Pomo community has land in Redwood Valley. There are several other Pomo communities, such as the one found at Yokaya, that have not been granted the status of reservations.

Across their old homeland, both on and off reservations, ancient customs continue to play an important part in native communities. Family life continues to be the focus of many traditions. Large numbers of young people are learning their ancient languages. They participate in traditional activities, such as dancing, singing, storytelling, basket making, and cooking. Pomo artwork is respected throughout the world. Native doctors continue to treat patients with ancient methods. Although they have preserved many of their traditions, the Pomo way of life has also grown and undergone changes. Many natives share religions with other Americans, such as Christianity and the Bahai faith.

This portrait of a Pomo man was taken in 1924.

54   This photo is of Ray Brown, Pomo Indian leader.

Just as there are many new promises, there are also new challenges for the Pomo. Despite all their efforts and victories, many Pomo are still denied the rights that are extended to other Native Americans and U.S. citizens. The Pomos' ancient homeland continues to be developed by, and for the benefit of, others. Their sacred places and sites are often destroyed to create new places for outsiders to live or work.

The Pomo nation deserves the respect and admiration of all the peoples of the modern world. They represent an example of the human experience that everyone can acknowledge and try to learn from.

Timeline

13,000–40,000 years ago	The ancestors of the Pomo arrive in North America from Asia.
8,000 years ago	The ancestors of the Pomo move into the coastal areas of California.
1542	Juan Rodriguez Cabrillo and his sailors pass by the Pomo area.
1769	The first Spanish colonists invade California.
1812	Russians establish Fort Ross in the Kashaya country.
1817	Mission San Rafael is founded. Some Pomo move south to join the mission.
1821	Mexico becomes independent of Spain.
1823	Mission San Francisco Solano de Sonoma is founded. Some Pomo people move to the outpost.

1833–1835	The Mexican government orders the elimination of the missions. During the decade that follows, increasing numbers of Pomo are forced to work at the Mexican ranches that are created in their territory, and Native Americans from Oregon carry off other Native Americans to make them slaves.
1841	The Russians decide to abandon Fort Ross. They sell the outpost to Mexican officials.
1848	The United States takes over California.
1850	The United States Cavalry slaughters hundreds of Pomo in a number of places, including Bloody Island.
1850–1900	The state and federal governments pass numerous laws that deny Native Americans their basic human rights. Most Pomos are forced to work for small amounts of pay on newcomers' farms.
1851–1860	The first detailed descriptions of the Pomo groups are provided by American settlers.
1870–1880	Many Pomo adopt the Ghost Dance religious movement.

1907	Ethan Anderson sues for the right to vote.
1910	The United States government begins to create small reservation communities at the *rancherías*.
1924	All Native Americans are made United States citizens.
1949–1970	Native Americans lose various rights as a result of new government policies. Community leaders resist and are partially successful in delaying or stopping some of the worst effects of the new policies.
1960– today	The Pomo continue to fight for their rights and play an important part in the Native American civil rights movement.

Glossary

bedrock mortars (BED-rok MOR-tuhrz)   Rock faces with holes that were used to grind seed and nuts into flour.

bola (BOHL-ah)   A hunting device made up of a piece of rope or leather that has a weight tied to each end. When thrown, it twists in the air and can knock down birds.

breechcloth (BREECH-klawth)   A kind of clothing made from a single piece of cloth or skin that is passed between the legs and tied at both ends to a belt.

chief (CHEEF)   A kind of leader who receives special privileges and redistributes goods to his people.

culture (KUHL-chuhr)   Shared, learned behavior.

dialect (DYE-uh-lekt)   A way of speaking a language found among a particular people or in a particular place. People who speak dialects of the same language may, or may not, be able to understand one another.

hematite (HEE-mah-tyt)   A mineral that can be used to make red paint.

hoppers (HAW-puhrz)   Bottomless baskets that were used to contain flour as it was being ground with a stone mortar.

Madunda (MUH-doon-dah)   A Pomo god who lived in the sky.

magnesite (MAG-nuh-syt)   A type of red stone that the Pomo used to make beads.

missions (MIH-shuhnz)   In colonial California, a kind of Spanish settlement where Native Americans were to be transformed into Christian citizens.

mortars (MOR-turz)   Circular holes in rocks that were used to crack nuts and grind seeds into flour.

obsidian (uhb-SIH-dee-uhn)   A kind of naturally occurring volcanic glass.

pendants (PEN-duhnts)   A type of jewelry suspended on a cord worn around the neck.

pestles (PEHS-tuhlz)   Cylindrical-shaped pieces of rocks used with mortars.

rancheria (ranch-eh-REE-ah)   A Spanish word that originally meant "a village made up of spread-out houses." This term continues to be used for all kinds of Pomo communities.

social structure (SOH-shul STRUHK-chur)   The way a community is divided into different groups of people.

tribelet (TRIBE-let)   A term sometimes used by anthropologists for what the Pomo considered to be their village communities.

Resources

BOOKS

Allen, Elsie. *Pomo Basketmaking: A Supreme Art for the Weaver.* Happy Camp, CA: Naturegraph Publishers, 1972.

Brown, Vinson. *Pomo Indians of California and Their Neighbors.* Happy Camp, CA: Naturegraph Publishers, 1969.

Campbell, Paul Douglas. *Survival Skills of Native California.* Salt Lake City, UT: Gibbs Smith, 1999.

Gibson, James R. *Imperial Russia in Frontier America.* New York: Oxford University Press, 1976.

Malinowski, Sharon (editor). *Gale Encyclopedia of Native American Tribes* (volume three). Detroit, MI: Gale Group, 1998.

MUSEUMS

California State Indian Museum
2618 K Street
Sacramento, CA 95816
(916) 324-0971
This museum presents the story of all of California's native people and has a large collection of Pomo materials.

Lake Mendocino Army Corps of Engineers Interpretive Center
1160 Lake Mendocino Drive
Ukiah, CA 95482-9404
(707) 462-7581
The Coyote Valley Pomo make presentations here.

Sonoma State Historic Park
20 East Spain Street
Sonoma, CA 95476
(707) 938-1519
The park preserves the remains of one of the missions where Pomo people made their home.

WEB SITES

Due to the changing nature of Internet links, PowerKids Press has developed an online list of Web sites related to the subject of this book. This site is updated regularly. Please use this link to access the site:

www.powerkidslinks.com/lna/pomo

Index